DEDICATED TO MY GRANDCHILDREN,

Hayden Koch and Preston Koch

I will always treasure the time we have spent together.

HYDRAULICS

FOR KIDS

By James Koehntopp

Many machines and tools harness the power of hydraulics to do simple work such as lifting, pushing, or pressing. Objects you see every day, like farm equipment, construction equipment, airplanes, and automobiles, use hydraulic energy.

Hydraulics is sometimes called fluid power because it uses energy from fluids to power the equipment. Pressurized hydraulic fluid is pumped through tubes and hoses to components such as cylinders or hydraulic motors that can perform work. Oil is most commonly used as the fluid because it does not compress under pressure and oil acts as a lubricant for moving parts.

In the next few pages, you will see many examples of how people use hydraulics. In the last part of the book, you will have the opportunity of creating a working hydraulics project.

A simple hydraulic jack can lift a heavy beam.

This jack weighs 20 pounds. With hydraulic pressure, the jack can lift a beam that weighs 40,000 pounds. A worker would not be able to lift a beam of that weight by hand, but with the help of hydraulics, he/she can lift it just by pumping the jack handle.

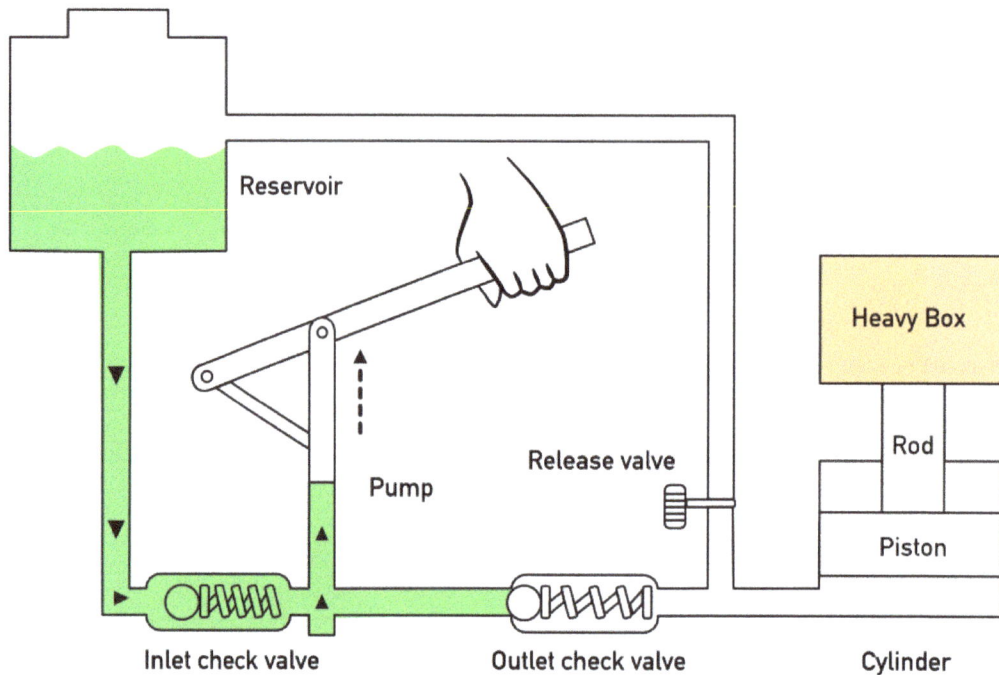

Reservoir

Release valve

Heavy Box

Rod

Pump

Piston

Inlet check valve

Outlet check valve

Cylinder

How a hydraulic jack fills oil into pump

When the pump handle is lifted, oil is drawn from the reservoir, past the inlet check valve then into the space created by the rising pump position.

Hydraulic Jack Components

Reservoir - Container to store the oil.

Inlet check valve - Allows oil to pass in one direction only and blocks any attempt for oil to flow back.

Pump - Draws oil in and then pushes the oil out of pump because of pumping strokes.

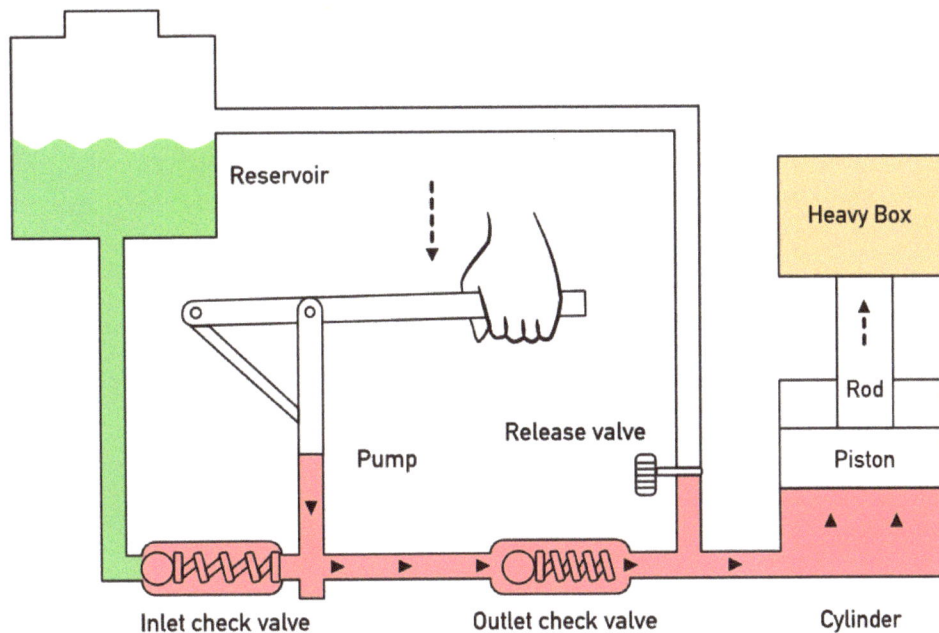

How a hydraulic jack lifts the load

When the pump handle is pushed down, oil is forced out of the pump, past the outlet check valve, and into the cap end of the cylinder, where it pushes the piston and rod up. The pump creates oil flow, while any load on the piston and rod builds hydraulic pressure.

Outlet check valve - Allows oil to pass in one direction only, Blocks any attempt to flow back regardless of the load on the cylinder.

Cylinder - Converts oil energy into mechanical movement. The piston and rod inside the cylinder move out, which lifts the heavy load. Oil under pressure can lift a load or push in order to do work.

Release valve - Opening the release valve allows oil in the cylinder to drain back to the reservoir, thus permitting the piston and rod to return to the bottom of the cylinder.

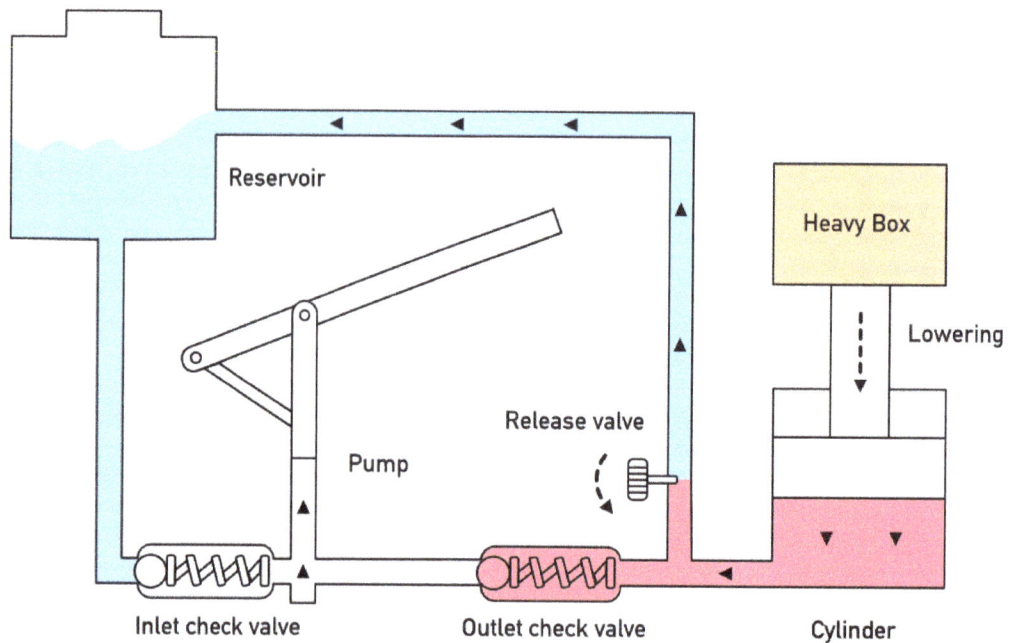

Reservoir

Heavy Box

Lowering

Release valve

Pump

Inlet check valve

Outlet check valve

Cylinder

How a hydraulic jack lowers the load

To lower the jack, the operator turns the release valve open. Opening the release valve allows trapped oil to leave thus allowing the piston and rod to lower. As the piston and rod are lowered, the load (heavy box) goes down.

Hydraulics in machinery

Auto mechanics need to get underneath cars to fix them. A car lift uses hydraulics to raise a car to a height that makes it easy to work on the underside of a vehicle.

Construction sites are full of hydraulics in action. For example, a front loader can easily lift and dump a heavy load of dirt or rocks. The driver sits in the cab and controls the loader's arms. Hydraulic cylinders lift the loader's arms and change the position of the bucket.

Large dump trucks are used to haul sand, dirt, gravel, and other materials to a job site. When the driver is ready to dump the load, he or she operates a lever that activates the hydraulic cylinder. The hydraulics lift the front of the box so that the material inside empties out the rear. A large dump truck can carry loads of 20,000 pounds or more. That is equal to the weight of five cars!

A crane is a tall machine with a long metal arm. It can lift materials into place while constructing a tall building. The crane operator controls the arm, which uses hydraulic power.

A scissors lift can also be used during the construction of buildings. Hydraulic cylinders squeeze the scissors' frames apart, forcing the platform upward. Can you see why they call it a scissors lift?

Many things are too heavy for people to lift. A forklift can lift, carry, and stack cargo. It is typically used to load products into a semi-trailer to transport to another location. Forklifts, which are sometimes called lift trucks, are used in shipyards, airports, warehouses, and more.

Workers use hydraulic machines to lift, pull, or push heavy things. It is important that the machine is operated in a safe manner by a responsible operator to prevent an accident or injury.

Hydraulic power is not just used for construction and automotive repair shops. Lots of everyday objects use hydraulic power.

Have you ever seen a chair like this in a hair salon or barber shop? This is another example of hydraulics in action. The lever on the side of the chair base allows the hair stylist to raise or lower the customer for a more comfortable working height.

Did you know your family car or pickup truck uses hydraulics? The brakes use hydraulic force to slow down and stop the vehicle. When the driver wants to stop, he or she steps on the brake pedal. Hydraulic fluid will squeeze the brakes at the wheels and the vehicle will stop.

Hydraulic Disc Brake System

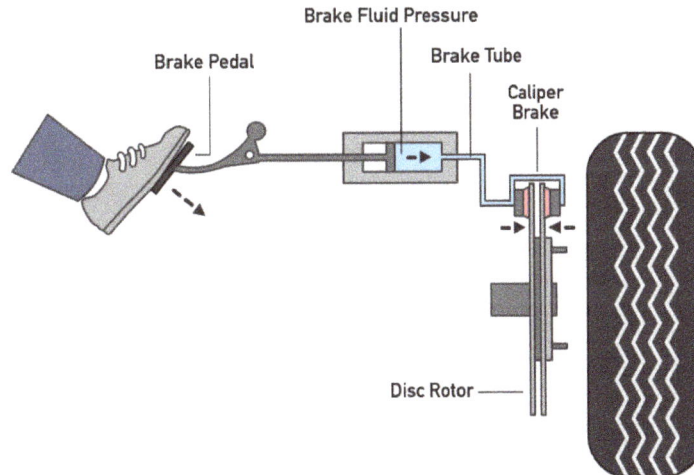

Brake Pedal

Brake Fluid Pressure

Brake Tube

Caliper Brake

Disc Rotor

Some elevators are operated by hydraulic pressure. They can raise and lower people in the elevator car.

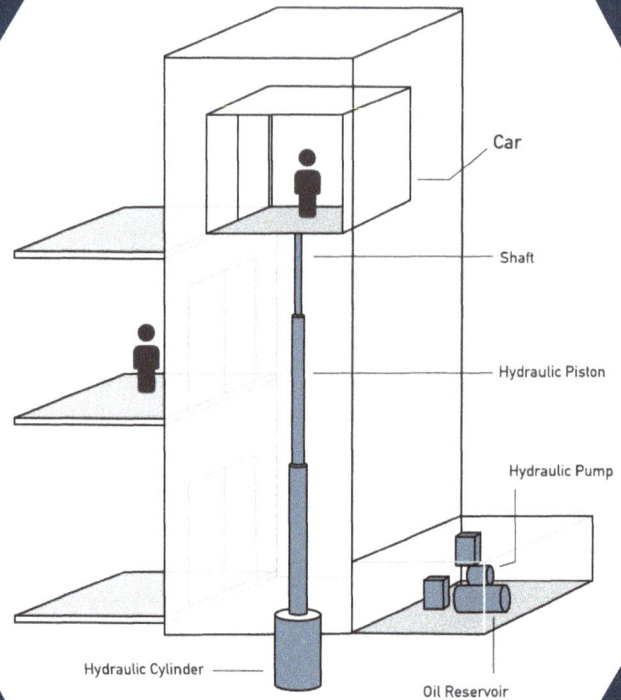

Car

Shaft

Hydraulic Piston

Hydraulic Pump

Hydraulic Cylinder

Oil Reservoir

Sometimes a tall boat needs to cross under a low bridge. A drawbridge can lift up to allow the boat to pass under it. Hydraulic power can harness enough energy to lift a steel and concrete bridge!

A bridge has a central span that is split into two leaves, called bascules. The leaves can be raised to allow river traffic to pass.

A worker, called a bridge tender, lifts and lowers the draw-bridge. A series of levers and massive gears raises the bridge using the power of hydraulics.

A portable hydraulic log splitter can be pulled behind a car or pickup truck to the job site. Using a hydraulic log splitter is much easier than splitting wood by hand with an ax. Logs can be lifted onto the splitter, then easily split into pieces for firewood with the push of a lever. Many machines using hydraulic force can be dangerous because they are so powerful. Proper training is important to prevent accidents.

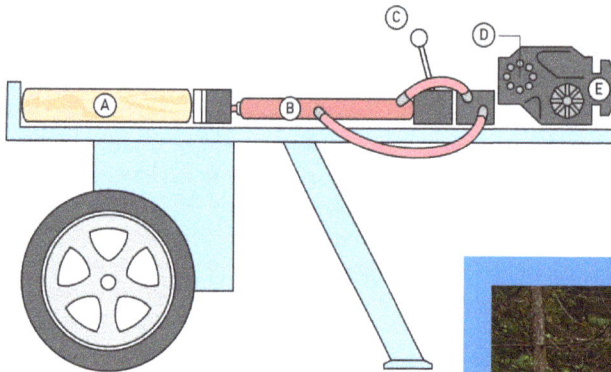

(A) Log
(B) Hydraulic Cylinder
(C) Directional Control Valve
(D) Hydraulic Pump
(E) Engine

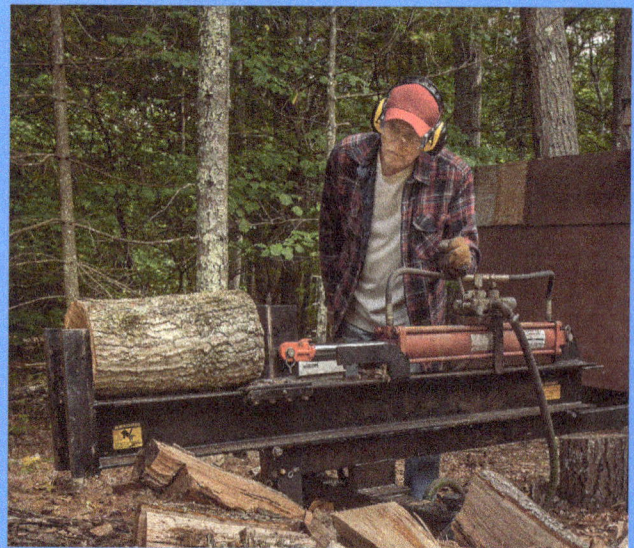

Reservoir

A reservoir is a container that holds the supply of oil. Oil is used because it doesn't compress like air, it doesn't freeze, and it lubricates the working parts.

Pump

The pump's job is to draw oil from the reservoir and push it into the hydraulic circuit. The pump is typically driven by an electric motor, gas engine, or diesel engine.

Cylinder

The cylinder receives the oil from the circuit and converts the oil under pressure into movement of the piston and rod. This is how work is accomplished.

Pressure Relief Valve

This is the safety valve for the system. If there is too much hydraulic pressure, this valve opens up, allowing oil to return back to the reservoir. This valve limits hydraulic pressure to a safe level.

Directional Valve

This valve directs the oil within the hydraulic circuit. When the operator moves the valve one way, oil is sent to the cap-end of the cylinder, thus making the rod move out. When the operator moves the valve the other way,

oil is sent to the rod—end of the cylinder, thus making the rod move back into the cylinder.

Oil Filter

The job of the filter is to clean the oil of wear particles that can cause harm to the hydraulic system.

Hydraulic components, explained

The pump draws oil from the reservoir and pushes it toward the directional valve. The directional valve position (as shown below) directs pressure oil to the cap-end of the hydraulic cylinder. Pressure oil then forces the piston and rod out of the cylinder to do work.

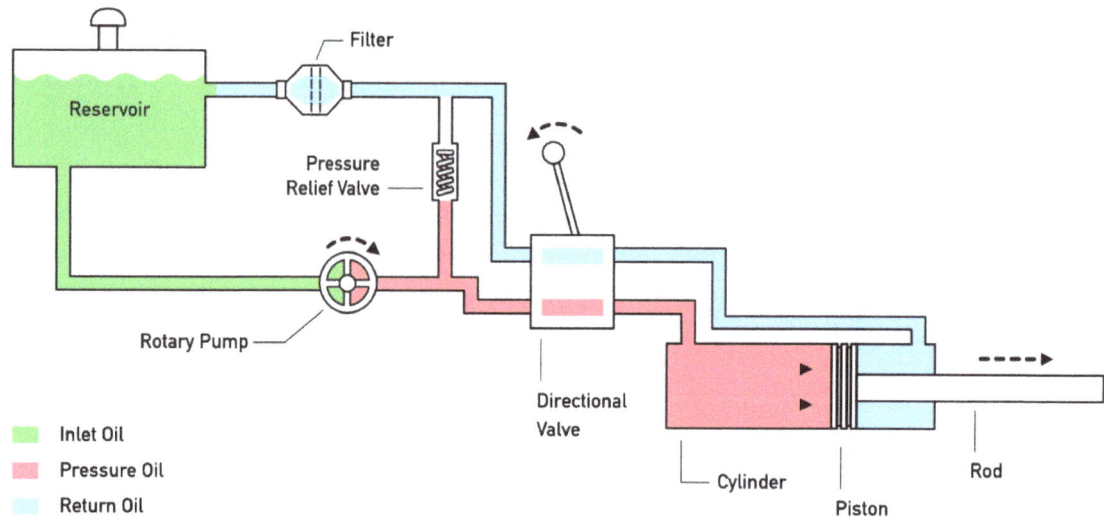

When the operator moves the handle of the directional valve to the opposite position, the oil flow takes a different path. The oil flow crosses and the pressure oil is now directed to the rod end of the cylinder. This causes the piston and rod to retract into the cylinder.

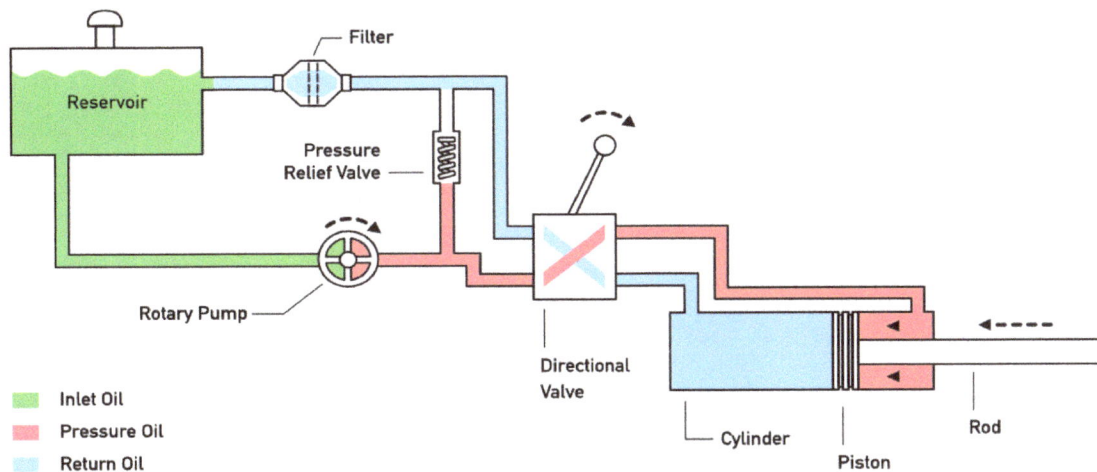

Filter

Reservoir

Pressure Relief Valve

Rotary Pump

Directional Valve

Cylinder

Piston

Rod

Inlet Oil

Pressure Oil

Return Oil

A factory press uses a hydraulic ram or cylinder to apply force to metal so that parts are pushed together or pushed apart. Pressure from hydraulics can also bend material to the proper shape.

As you can see, hydraulic applications are all around us. From simple machines to heavy equipment, hydraulic power can get the job done. Hydraulic theory and basic hydraulic machines have been around for hundreds of years and are still used today.

These are a few occupations that use hydraulics. Do you have any friends or family members with these jobs?

Tractor Operator	Firefighter
Truck Driver	Miner
Auto Technician	Factory Worker
Heavy Equipment Operator	Well Driller
Construction Worker	Warehouse Worker
Heavy Equipment Technician	Garbage Hauler
Farmer	Aircraft Technician

Can you think of any other jobs that use hydraulics?

Questions

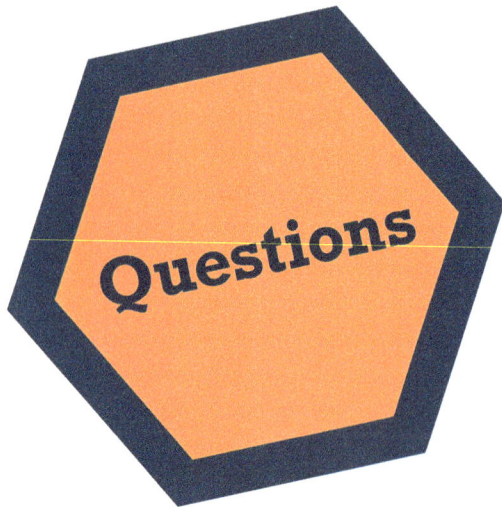

1. Which item does not use hydraulics?

    A. Crane
    B. Dump Truck
    C. Wheel Barrow

2. What type of fluid does most hydraulic-powered equipment use?

    A. Water
    B. Oil
    C. Engine Coolant

3. What allows a hydraulic jack ram to return to its lower position slowly?

    A. Moving the hand pump up and down slowly
    B. Waiting for ram to release on its own
    C. Opening release valve slowly

4. A car lift is used to:

    A. Change tires
    B. Wash the vehicle
    C. Fill the gas tank

5. What is a front-end loader used for?

    A. To lift workers to the roof of a building
    B. To load dirt and sand into a truck box
    C. To carry a pallet of drywall to another location

6. What is a dump truck used for?

    A. To carry waste water
    B. To transport sand, dirt, or rocks to
       another location
    C. To transport people in a local parade

7. What type of hydraulic machinery would be used to lift a steel beam into place?

    A. Forklift
    B. Scissors Lift
    C. Crane

8. What causes the car brake fluid to become pressurized and push on the brake calipers?

    A. The driver's foot pushing on the
       brake pedal.
    B. The tires making contact with
       the road.
    C. The car going really fast.

9. What occupation does not typically use hydraulics?

    A. Barber
    B. Truck mechanic
    C. Farmer
    D. Librarian
    E. Construction worker

Answers:

9: D Librarian

8: A The drivers foot pushing on the brake pedal.

7: C Crane

6: B To transport sand, dirt, or rocks to another location

5: B To load dirt and sand in to a truck box

4: A Change tires

3: C Open release valve

2: B Oil

1: C Wheel Barrow

Experience hydraulics in action! On the next few pages, there are several hydraulic projects you can build with the help of an adult.

Building a Hydraulic Press:

Refer to the sketch of a press project shown on the next page. Use the sketch to determine the materials needed.

On a wooden base, glue (2) upright beams. Next, glue (2) tongue depressors on one side of upright beams. The tongue depressors act as side supports. Glue press ram (syringe 2) vertically onto the inside of side supports. After the syringe is glued in place, the remaining side supports can be glued in place on the opposite side of upright beams.

Attach piston pump syringe to the press ram syringe using plastic hose and fill the pump syringe with water. When the piston pump is pushed, the fluid will travel through the hose to the press ram/actuating cylinder. The plunger of the press ram (syringe 2) will hydraulically lower with enough force to squash a grape or small item.

Caution: Have an adult help you with the hot glue gun.

Hydraulic Press Project

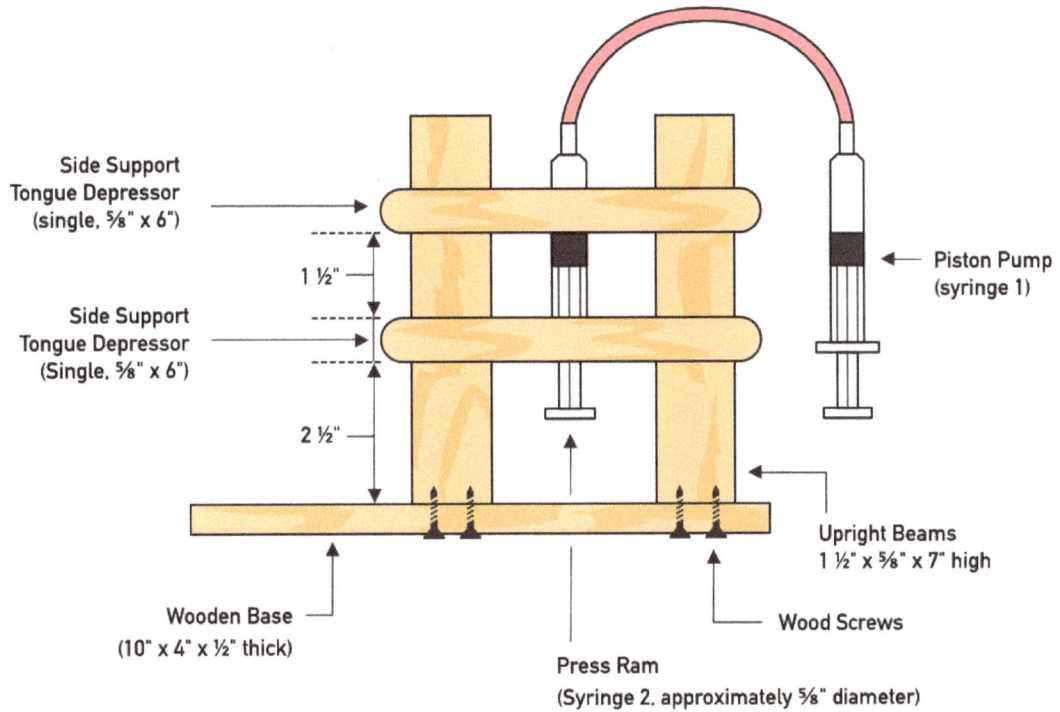

Side Support
Tongue Depressor
(single, ⅝" x 6")

Side Support
Tongue Depressor
(Single, ⅝" x 6")

1 ½"

2 ½"

Piston Pump
(syringe 1)

Upright Beams
1 ½" x ⅝" x 7" high

Wooden Base
(10" x 4" x ½" thick)

Press Ram
(Syringe 2, approximately ⅝" diameter)

Wood Screws

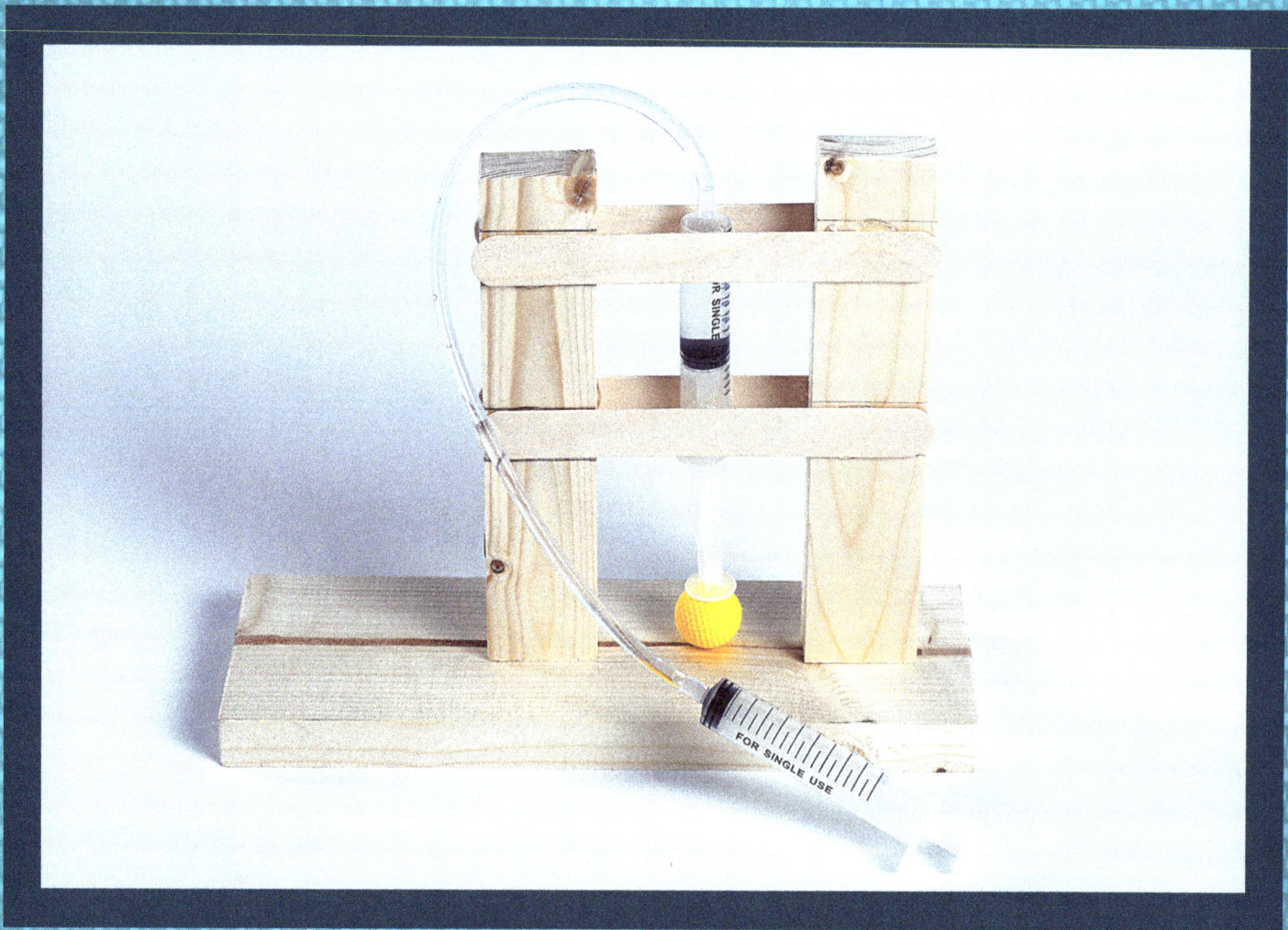

Hydraulic Scissors Lift Project

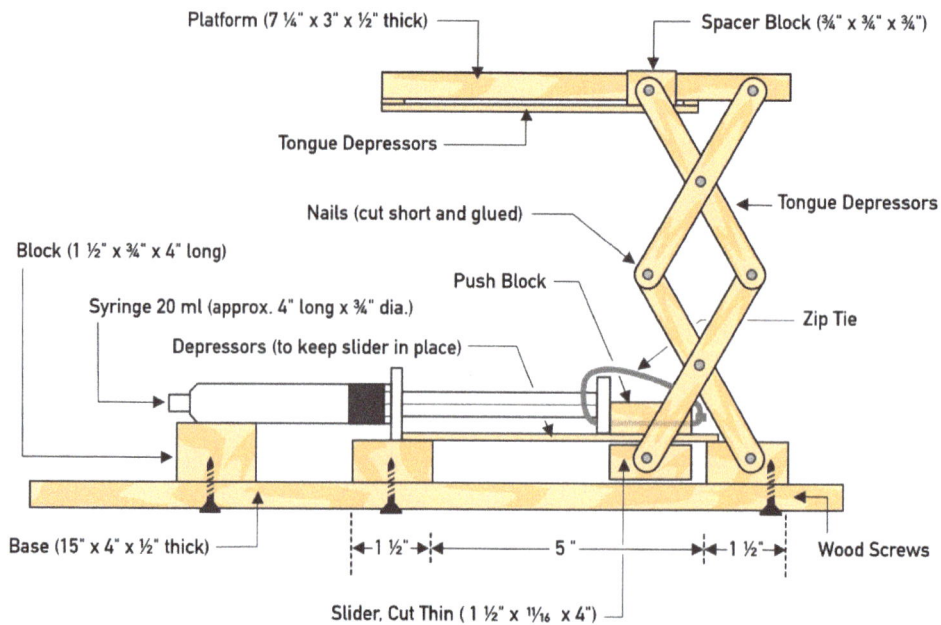

Platform (7 ¼" x 3" x ½" thick)

Spacer Block (¾" x ¾" x ¾")

Tongue Depressors

Tongue Depressors

Nails (cut short and glued)

Push Block

Block (1 ½" x ¾" x 4" long)

Syringe 20 ml (approx. 4" long x ¾" dia.)

Depressors (to keep slider in place)

Zip Tie

Base (15" x 4" x ½" thick)

⊢ 1 ½" ⊣ 5 " ⊢ 1 ½" ⊣

Wood Screws

Slider, Cut Thin (1 ½" x ¹¹⁄₁₆ x 4")

Building a Scissors Lift:

On a wooden base, screw (or glue) in place (2) 1 ½" x ¾" blocks. Next, cut a 1" x 1" x 4" (or as size dictates) block to support the base end of the pump syringe. Also, cut a wood block 1 ½" x 11/16" x 4". This block needs to be thinner so that it can slide easily between the base and tongue depressors that are to be glued to the top of the base blocks.

Drill holes into (8) tongue depressor to make the scissors pieces. Use aluminum nails cut very short to insert in the (4) hinges of the scissors pieces on each side. Screws will be used on the top (2) and bottom (2) scissors ends. Hot glue the cut-off nail ends.

On the underside of the platform, glue spacers (shims) to provide an air gap between the platform and the depressors. The air gap allows a cross bar between the platform and depressors to slide freely.

Fasten scissors' ends to platform and base with wood screws (do not over-tighten screws.)

Glue actuator syringe to blocks with hot glue gun. Drill a hole in the syringe pushing end and the push block, then fasten with a zip tie.

Mount the pump syringe on the base if desired. This pump will be filled with water and connected by a hose to the actuating cylinder.

When you push on the pump syringe, the pressurized fluid will travel through the hose to the actuator syringe, which will exert force on the push block. This, in turn, will cause the push block with slider to move towards the end block. This movement causes the scissors-like action and the platform will rise.

Caution: Have an adult help you with the hot glue gun.

Hydraulic Drawbridge Project

Building a Hydraulic Drawbridge

Refer to the sketches of this project shown on the next pages and use them to determine the materials needed. Assemble tongue depressors side-by-side for the length of the 16" bridge deck. Mark where the ⅛" thick x 1" inner supports will be glued, then glue in place. Next, build an upper deck as truss design or flats. This can be built similar to the lower deck, but only 11" long. At this time, you can drill holes through the supports and the upper and lower decks and gently bolt the pieces together. Next, build two under bridge supports. One will be a rectangular block, while the other block needs to be cut into an H-shape to support the hydraulic syringe (cylinder). This end will be affixed to the hinge end of the lower deck. Attach a cylinder support to the underside of the lower deck. Use plastic zip ties as hinges and as attachments to the ends of the syringe (cylinder).

Next, mount a pump (syringe) on the base if desired. This pump will be filled with water and connected by a hose or tube to the actuating cylinder (syringe). When you push on the pump (syringe), the fluid will travel through the hose to the actuating cylinder (syringe) with sufficient force to lift the bridge.

Bridge Truss
Side View

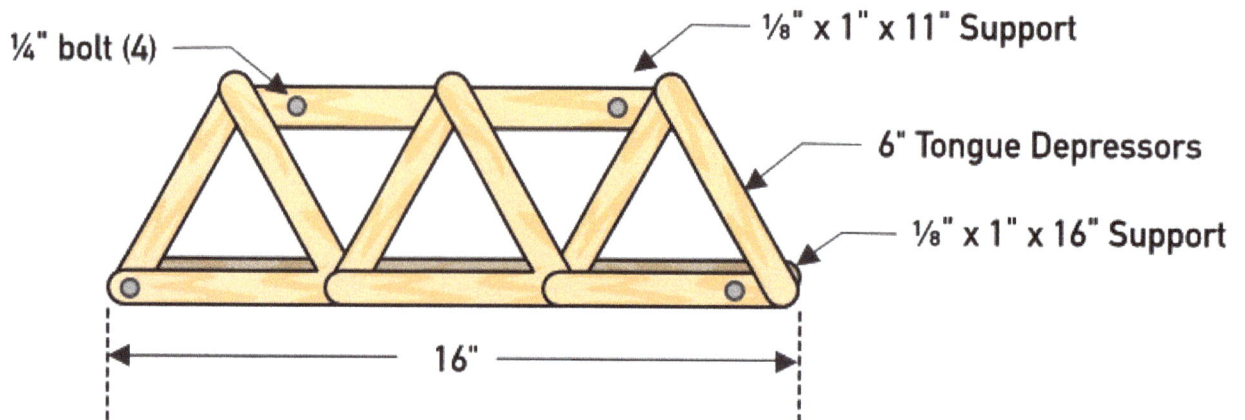

¼" bolt (4)

⅛" x 1" x 11" Support

6" Tongue Depressors

⅛" x 1" x 16" Support

16"

Bridge Deck
Top View

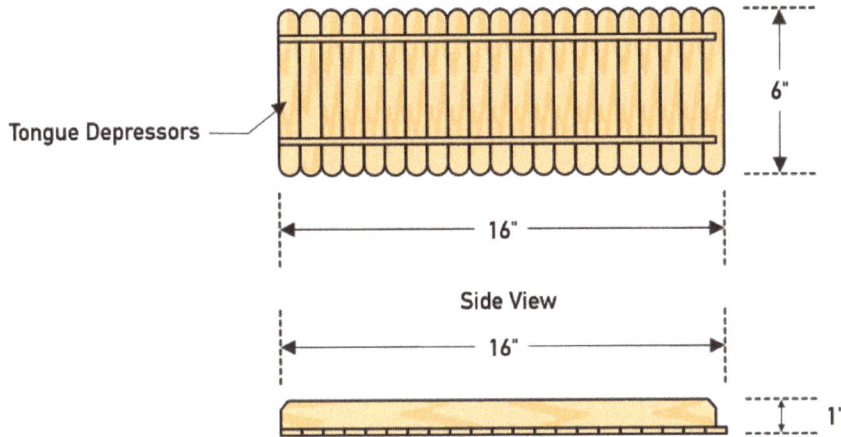

Tongue Depressors

6"

16"

Side View

16"

1"

Under BridgeSupport - Anchor End

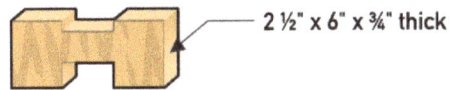

2 ½" x 6" x ¾" thick

Cylinder Support

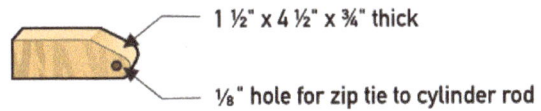

1 ½" x 4 ½" x ¾" thick

⅛" hole for zip tie to cylinder rod

Shop Crane Project

Building a Long-Reach Shop Crane:

This working project illustrates a shop crane, which is a common repair tool used in vehicle repair shops to remove or install engines.

Use a pair of 21" long paint stir sticks for the long lift arm and a pair of 12" paint stir sticks for the uprights. The wooden base measures ¾" x 3 ½" x 20". The lift arm pieces are hot glued with 1" wooden spacer blocks between them. The uprights are hot glued with 1 ½" wooden spacer blocks between them. The angle braces are a pair of 6" long tongue depressors. The lifting ram (sometimes called cylinder) uses a 20 ml veterinary syringe installed under the lift arm. The piston pump (another 20 ml syringe) connects to the ram with plastic hose. When the circuit is filled with water, the ram will lift a small object when the piston pump is pushed.

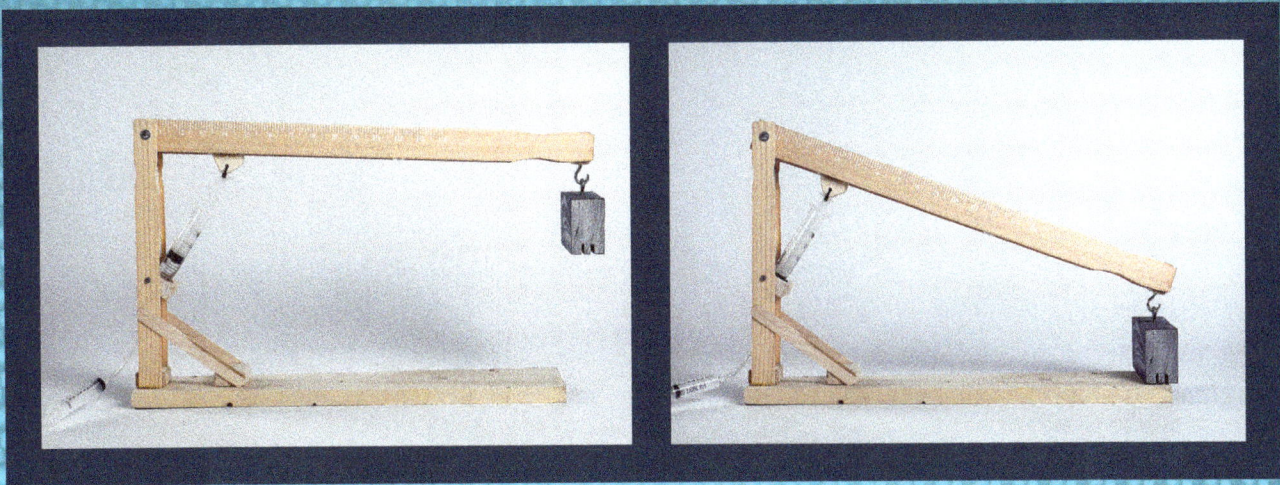

Shop Crane Project

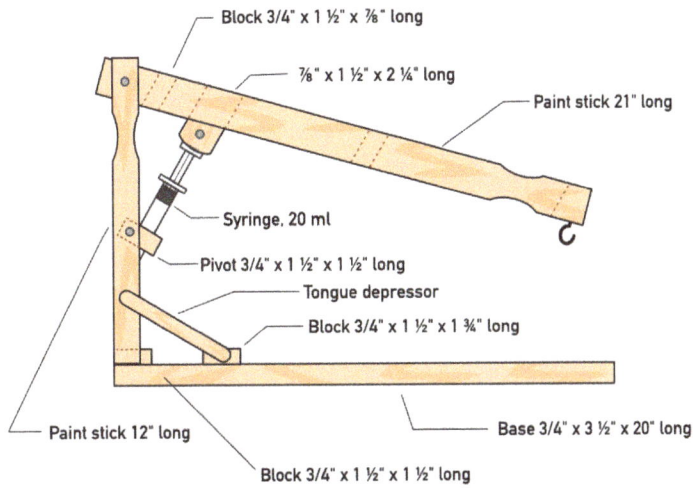

Block 3/4" x 1 ½" x ⅞" long

⅞" x 1 ½" x 2 ¼" long

Paint stick 21" long

Syringe, 20 ml

Pivot 3/4" x 1 ½" x 1 ½" long

Tongue depressor

Block 3/4" x 1 ½" x 1 ¾" long

Paint stick 12" long

Base 3/4" x 3 ½" x 20" long

Block 3/4" x 1 ½" x 1 ½" long

Hydraulic Lid Project

Building a hydraulic operated lid

Materials Needed: basket, basket lid (made of tongue depressors) 1 plastic syringe (12 ml) to serve as a pump. 1 plastic syringe (12 ml) to serve as an actuating cylinder. 1 ft. plastic tubing to serve as piping.

Refer to the sketch on the next page. Find or build a basket of your choosing. Build a lid by gluing tongue depressors together with supporing ties, using a hot glue gun or liquid glue.

Use zip ties for hinges and connectors. Attach plastic tubing to pump (filled with water) and to the actuator, which is now attached to the basket and lid at the hinge end.

When you depress the pump syringe, the fluid will travel to the actuating syringe, forcing the lid of the basket to open like magic.

Caution: Have an adult help you with the hot glue gun.

Hydraulic Lid Project
for basket

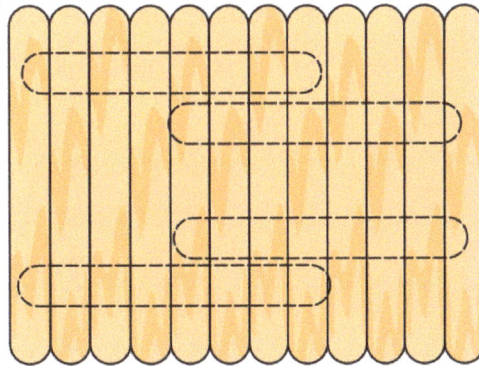

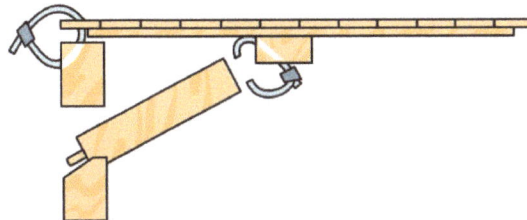

Acknowledgement

A special thank you to Terika Koch

Book designed by Melvin Grefalda
Stock images by: Shutterstock and Adobe Stock
Additional photography by Amy McManigal

www.ingramcontent.com/pod-product-compliance
Lightning Source LLC
Chambersburg PA
CBHW040248100426
42811CB00011B/1193